A Satisfactory Daughter

The poet and her mother, Rita Julius, circa 1947.
Photo by the poet's father, William R. Julius.

A Satisfactory Daughter

Jane Julius Honchell

NYQ Books™

The New York Quarterly Foundation, Inc.
New York, New York

NYQ Books™ is an imprint of The New York Quarterly Foundation, Inc.

The New York Quarterly Foundation, Inc.
P. O. Box 2015
Old Chelsea Station
New York, NY 10113

www.nyq.org

First Edition

Set in New Baskerville

Layout by Raymond P. Hammond

Cover Design by Raymond P. Hammond

Cover Art: "Glacial," 20" x 24" prismacolor and ink on bristol, © 2008
    by Amy Honchell | www.amyhonchell.com

Cover Art Photo by Jeremy Thomas Handrup

Author Photo by Kassidy Evans Kraky

Library of Congress Control Number: 2017947451

ISBN: 978-1-63045-030-4

A Satisfactory Daughter

Acknowledgments

Some of the poems in this volume have been, or will be, published in: *The New York Quarterly*; *Five Poets* (Nightshade Press); *Palpable Clock: 25 years of Mulberry Poets* (University of Scranton Press) and *Down the Dog Hole: 11 Poets on Northeast Pennsylvania* (Nightshade Press).

Special thanks to everyone who helped in the birthing of this book:

To Keystone College, for the semester sabbatical award that provided precious time to write. To my devoted band of first readers for their astute comments, suggestions, and patient attention, especially Amy Honchell, Tim Joyce, and Bill and Mandy Honchell, and my Writers' Group: David and Carolyn Elliott, Laurel Radzieski, Brian Fanelli, Michael Huff, Robert Dugan, Kristie Ridilla, and Macaulay Glynn. To Justin Kraky and Kassidy Evans Kraky, for their technical and artistic support. To Raymond Hammond, Editor-in-Chief of NYQ Books, for his belief in my work and supreme patience. To Amanda Bradley, fellow traveler, and to Bob Fox, for asking the right questions. Finally, thanks to my students, past and present, who inspire, teach, and delight me.

Contents

I. The Apple of Her Eye

II. *Seasonings*

III. *On Looking into* Gray's Anatomy

In memory of my parents,
Bill and Rita Julius,

and to

Amy and Bill,
the most satisfactory children a mother could desire.

A Satisfactory Daughter

Entering Wonderland

The mother of invention curls her finger, beckoning,
says *Come in, the door is open.* So follow
directions, uncork the bottle and slug it down.
Let the astonishment of pond frogs transformed
to footmen invite you to read a new language
in your calico's smile. Discover metaphor's
alchemy in flamingo mallets and inspect

the shattered egg of tragedy. Allow yourself
to celebrate all—from the little chipping
sparrow's trill to the stars' magnificent arias.
Just throw back your head and sing *O frabjous day!*
Calloo! Callay! It's a simple opening wide,
this business of drinking in everything,
of living in wonder.

I. The Apple of Her Eye

Babies Hospital, 1947

When we are gone—a generation bottle-fed
on Doctor Spock's strict schedule,
no matter how loudly our hunger howled
while our mothers wept to hear,
but waited until the clock ticked down
to hold us—

when we are gone, no one will be left
who can still smell in dreams the cloying scent
of ether pressed in metal masks over faces
there, on the cold steel table, or recollect our sense
of suffocation and unpalliated
terror,

or who will always define loneliness as endless
weeks when only starched strangers
fed and bathed us, hurt us with instruments
lifted from covered enamel trays (No
visitors permitted except on weekends, one
hour a day),

or who remembers when our parents
made the long trip by train or car
to our bedsides to gift and kiss
us, or how we all, grown and small,
pretended happiness, waited until we were alone
to cry,

or who recalls how, in the night-light's watery
glow, cribbed in the hushed ward, we took
comfort in the radio's hum, William
Tell's Overture announcing the Lone Ranger's
coming, his hearty *Hi-yo Silver, Away!*
promising rescue.

The Best Kiss

Nothing—not the eyelash tickle
of an Eskimo kiss, your first kiss's
dry-mouthed clumsiness, nor tongues
twining like hot snakes—comes close
to the moment your mother's cool
lips brushed and soothed your hot
forehead as you sank into sleep.

Original Sin

I learn guilt, the fall from grace, at three, eating
red raspberries unbidden from our neighbor's garden.
So many times I'd followed Mrs. Spears down sun-warmed
rows, picking peas and bush beans, pulling scallions,
that I never dreamed it wrong to help myself to riches.

When mommy asks if the ruby caps staining
my lips were gifts, and I say no, she elects
to nip sin in the bud. The words *you stole*
sting and burn, and I'm made to go, alone,
to confess my theft, shame flaming my cheeks.

Though forgiven, told I'm always welcome,
the woman's kind remission can't cool
that heat, restore my innocence. Tainted now,
her garden's joys are lost to me. Even today,
I push raspberries to the side of my plate.

The Stanislavski Method

Learning to read—
See Jane run. Run, Jane, run!
like deliberately spaced droplets hitting me
right between the eyes—
was interminable torture.
Words and their meanings
seemed to crouch
on opposite sides of a great divide
I couldn't bridge,
reading just another item
on my list of the unmastered:
tying shoes, subtracting, being good.

My actress mother turned the light on,
taught me Stanislavski's *Magic If*—
to speak as if there were a reason
for Jane's perpetual running.
Be afraid for her, she coached,
and seeing now the dark and tangled
monster breathing at my own back,
Run, Jane! Run! I screamed.

Next day, when we worst readers
circled our chairs like covered wagons
against marauding hordes
and my turn came,
Jane fled for her life across the page.
Miss Grimaldi thought somehow I'd cheated,
and so I read on and on,
the words pouring out in unstoppable streams,
gathering speed. Twirling in their current
I swam at last in that ecstatic amnion
where words and meaning live.

Never-Never Land

Fourth graders are all the same, avid
as cadaver dogs to sniff out difference,
quick to sense the invisible ash on a sacrificial
forehead and mean as snakes.
But Gracella French, who bore the stigmata
of poor on her hand-me-down dresses, carried
the taint of her father's work draining cesspools,
just flitted among us: oblivious, gypsy-haired shadow.

When her invitation arrived, I cried,
but mother made me go, drove to the house
where the wind whispered *lonely* and flailed
paint to the bone, ripped petals from roses planted
in an old tractor tire there in the weed-clotted yard.
Only three of us showed. Yet when Gracella
unbowed my package of plastic barrettes,
she glowed as if I'd given her treasure.

I remember best her home's alien air,
its acrid, metallic scent stinging my nose.
That, and the lopsided chocolate cake
her mother baked from scratch, frosted
in neon green exactly the shade of the poisoned
cake Captain Hook gave Peter Pan.
Expecting death at any moment, I ate a slice
like Tinkerbelle, my small atonement.

But now I know that reason is a lie,
for as she passed our plates, Gracella's mother
paused and stroked her daughter's hair
with such hot love, such glistening pride,
I wanted to eat that too.

Facts of Life

We move to the country when I turn ten, and I find
a friend in Melanie (named for Scarlet
O'Hara's best friend). We hang out in the cellar
where they live for years while Mr. Campbell raises
the new house above them. Some nights, we girls
pajama party in the den, with its bearskin
rug, huge-headed, smelly, its red tongue
lolling so hungrily I fear the beast
will rise in the night and savage me
as I sleep on the plaid couch. One day I watch

Karen (eight years old, face like a Christmas
angel) wring the necks of baby chicks too weak
to thrive as casually as you'd snap a twig.
Farm girl, she takes in stride bull mounting
heifer, foal's bloody birth, the necessity
of butchery so shocking to a city child.

She'll die at eighteen, neck broken when
her horse stumbles a cross-country jump
at Devon—just one more required sacrifice.

Two-part Harmony

In memory's green kitchen, sisters pay
the nightly price for dinner, spatting over dishes.
We can't live in unison, but to the plink and clash
of glassware, pots and pans, we harmonize to beat the band
on songs learned at camp, rounds, old hymns. Sally commandeers
the lead, my alto twines around and under, a cat
circling the shins of her melody. As the drain sucks
down the last gray suds, we always finish the job
with *Spirit of the Living God*, mom's favorite.
Too young to read the sex in its incantatory plea,
still it feels right to belt out *Melt me, mold me,*
use me, fill me in a passionate crescendo, then whisper
the hymn's refrain to the night.

The Best Memory

I remember the serenity of Sunday
mornings, there in the little room tucked
under the eaves. Propped up on pillows.
New York Times still unread and heavy
on my lap, coffee's dark notes flooding
my tongue, promise of bacon to come, radio
purring and you asleep, warming our bed,
your body a furnace in all weathers.

Maybe it snowed overnight, and I woke
to bright silence enfolding the world,
white mounds hiding its dirt. So pristine,
this snow-globe scene, this moment,
that my heart slows, breath lengthens
and I drift back to the dream we once were.

Too Late

Night falls, the ovened casserole hangs
on the cusp between crusty and succulent.
She refuses to cry, but her jib-jittering heart
flutters.
Pacing and pacing the hall, she tries
not to pull back the curtain again,

wonders *What keeps him from me*,
possibilities ticking down like a bomb:
simple forgetfulness (He never could tell
time.), a telephone call he can't end,
a woman sprawled across his desk?
Or did his car slip off the road,
press itself into the trunk of an oak?
Is he (unthinkable!) dead?

Then the bare twigs of worry rub
together, smoke, flame into fury.
How many more long nights
when the door stays closed so late
before she just stops caring?

Star-crossed

Natty in pin-striped pelt, white spats and bib immaculate,
Buster's every inch a gentleman. Instantly smitten by Lola's
springy showgirl gait and alluring pink asterisk beckoning
like a bull's-eye beneath raised tail, he bustles up to touch noses,
but she hisses catty imprecations, rakes him with a claw.

How could he know Lola is drawn only to the heat
of humans? Shameless in her need for touch,
she accosts the unwary on the john, leaping
onto complete strangers' laps, kneading and purring
her heart out. Even her meows sound like *Mama.*

Thus these cats will never meet at a masked ball,
pledge undying love from balconies, be pricked out
in little stars in the same constellation, nor in this life curl
in one furred circle, eat tuna from a common bowl,
though Buster pines and wishes otherwise.

Break-up

She's such a fickle bitch. One minute her humid breath
tickles your ear in dreams, the next, she's cooled,
flitted off to who knows where, leaving you empty
penned, exchanging blank stares with the page.
Useless to beg, cajole, rage, or ply with pathetically
wilted bouquets until your pores ooze blood.
She doesn't care. Some hunky poet laureate
or that woman with dandelion hair has snared her.

So just suck it up. Sharpen pencils, wash the roof,
read cheap thrillers, phone your shrink, fiddle
with the Sunday puzzle, eat a peach, maybe scream
a little. Pretend you never needed her. Tell friends
she was a lousy kisser and a slut. Then write a poem
about the lovely hussy you miss so much.

The best bread

for Joan Daniels

arrives at our door in the dead of night, cached
in black trash bags, fresh from Joan's kitchen,
just when I'm down to the last sleeve of saltines,
and payday's a week away. We've been living
on peanut butter and spongy Sunshine bread,
food of the heartsick and poor, too proud to beg,

but this bread, unbought and unasked,
is leavened with such tact we can eat
without feeling needy and beholden for alms.
In fact, it makes us feel rich. In its rye,
wheat and white, black pumpernickel,
poppyseeds and lemon zest, its crisp-crusted
eggy heft, such sustenance! We chew love,
nibble courage, inhale the yeasty scent of hope.

Still Looking

He's a big bear-hug of a man now, this son
with topaz eyes and his grandfather's laugh,
brain a-jangle with scurrying plans.
Little, he never slept, refused to take naps, climbed
out of his crib ready to start the day at 4 a.m. and crept
down the hall to stand at the side of my bed. When I feigned
sleep, he pried up my eyelid, asked *Are you in there?*
Mad as I was, I never could resist his saving sense of fun.

He never learned to ride a bike, but he was hell
on his Big Wheel, scattering dogs, old lady
strollers, the occasional nun, in his path. And thus
he careens through life—fast, impulsive, sometimes
rash, a master of words, but still feeling his way
in the dark toward a sleeping destiny.

We take hands

as we come to the room where her father lies
waiting, husk of his brain cracked by a stroke.
My girl and I reach out for each other
at the same moment, and again I'm amazed
by her hand, so small, so tenderly pliant.

One touch and forty years rewind, like newspaper
pages blurring a microfiche screen, to the instant
they place the hot bundle of her on my chest, and she
opens those cobalt eyes, stares into mine, assessing,
then twines the tiny starfish of her hand tight
around my thumb, claiming me.

But don't be deceived by their softness. Her hands
have a powerful grasp, have learned deftness,
precision. I've watched them sculpt cloth into intricate
folds, exactly the way she wants them to turn,
her touch unerringly true. And I've seen them coax
objects into submission, make pencils, piecrusts, bits
of glitter do whatever she says, bend them gently
to her will, the way they do with people, too.

Legacy

I coax my car to life
as snowflakes paste lace on windshield,
already late.
Five miles away, my daughter
steps on stage to sing.

White waves of snow billow back
nights I scanned crowds to find
my father, beaming, and
(as if I could have missed that radiance)
waving his white handkerchief message:
I love you. I am here.

Tonight as breath blinds the glass with ice,
I imagine Amy's big eyes
searching strangers' smiles for mine.
I slide into the No Parking, School Bus Only slot,
run bootless, gloveless through the drifts,
scale knees and laps, slump in breathless disarray.

Impaled by light, small white face
lifted, my firstborn raises her pure voice
to the hushed hall, heralding another birth, a star.
As her eyes still strain the dark,
I fumble purse and pocket, find
one tattered tissue,
wave and wave and wave.

American Gothic

It's easy to make fun of this long-faced,
pitchforked couple, but in old photographs
my great-great grandmother looks just like
Grant Woods' careworn woman, both of them pared
to the bone by toil, both rigid with occasion,
holding themselves upright by sheer will.
As if revealing feelings would be unseemly,
the painted woman and the real avoid the artist's
gaze, the camera's lens, stare into the middle distance,
turned inward, lips ironed into grim straight lines.

What sad meat the farmer's woman
eats, we can only guess, but I know
my ancestor's griefs, penned as they are
in our old family Bible in her rigid copperplate
hand, ink now the rusty color of old blood:
four babies dead before they turned three,
two within days, one gone on Christmas Eve,
Into the arms of God, she said. Their times on earth
so brief she listed them right down to the day.
No wonder she'd forgotten how to smile.

Not Far from the Tree

Empty acorn caps litter the ground
around the gazebo, but the few oak
leavings still uncrunched beneath
our boots are lovely: overlapping reptilian
scales flowering out from stems, concavities
smooth as polished hardwood floors,

and they take me back to grandpa, who hated
waste. He saved string, flattened and folded
candy wrapper tinfoil into tidy squares,
clipped straws in half, wrote lists on the backs
of unsent postcards with pencils sharpened
down to Lilliputian lengths. Behind his back,
grandma groused he was a bore, a fussy
pedant lacking imagination and romance,

but this quiet man of beige and gray
collected and shellacked the amber husks
that squirrels abandoned, crafting dollhouse cups
and bowls for me. And later, our heads bent
over kitchen table, showed me his stamp
collection. We turned the album pages slowly,
seeing in the etched images of presidents,
bi-planes, palm trees, butterflies, Romanian
bears, clipper ships and queens, all of human
history and worlds we'd travel only in dreams.

The Apple of Her Eye

When new friends cooed and patted my head,
mother said *Yes, she's a satisfactory daughter,*
loving the drama of their sharply indrawn breaths.

Like them, you might think her cruel, or that she feared
I'd spoil like a peach left in the sun of too much love,
or that satisfactory was parental modesty—

a little verbal finger-crossing to ward off the evil
eye that feeds on pride. And you could be right
on all counts. But I remembered my grammy

had called mom the same, and even then sensed
how words' chameleon meanings can change
color against green leaves or red, so I believed

she meant I'd turned out right, contented her
the way a rich meal sates appetite, that I
was not merely average, like a report card C,

and the anthem of her praise sang in my head.
I wore its approbation like Miss America's
tiara and never ceased trying to please.

My daughter's the same, and today I wonder
if this need to satisfy was bred in the bone,
a chromosomal prompting, some primordial

urge that made three generations of women
cleave to our dams so we could see our tiny
selves reflected in the apples of their eyes.

All I know for sure is this: when, at the end,
mother whispered *You have always been my*
satisfactory daughter, I too was satisfied.

The Chosen

This morning, so distracted by words (all raising
and waving their hands, clamoring for attention,
showing off, hot to be trotted out on the page)
I drove right past the grocery store
and had to turn back, refocus. Checking my list,
I found more words, already selected:
escarole, parsley, arugula, thyme, Yukon
Golds, wild-caught steelhead trout, cat chow,
frozen peas, ziti, Greek yogurt and Oreos lined
up in a row—utilitarian, spare, yet not without
a certain charm—all patiently waiting, secure
and a little smug, as only the elect can be.

Then, moved by the others' desperate pleas,
I relented, thought *Well perhaps just one more.*
Though tempted by paprika, flirting perkily
there in the front row, I chose instead the homely kid
nobody likes, slumped over his desk at the back of the room,
wrote *kumquat* on the last line.

Villanelle for the Faithful Ones

Bless all the creatures that mate forever,
egrets stalking the swamps in pairs,
my parents, united for worse and for better.

Imagine them happy, braving all weathers
like puffins clowning around without care.
Bless all these beings who mate forever.

Such a wonder they manage to stay together,
those bald eagles tending chicks in their aeries,
like my parents, nested for worse and for better.

Study the barn swallows feather by feather,
swooping in tandem, scything the air,
and bless all the strong ones that mate forever.

Just look at the trumpeter swans: no lever
can pry them apart, and then there's my parents,
mated, entwined, for worse or for better,

until one of them dies and the other, bereft, never
recovers, though she pretends to conquer despair.
So I bless all the creatures that mate forever,
especially my parents, for worse and for better.

Abandoned

Whether you sit by your father's bed
and see his breathing slow to a stutter, the lights
going out as he leaves his house, turning
the lock behind him, or you arrive too late
to wave goodbye and find no note on the table,
the result is the same: you're left with an empty
home whose shuttered windows and boarded up
doors forever keep you out in the cold.

No matter that you understand these leavings
are inevitable and right, you can't escape the wild
desire to take his hand, draw him back
to the warm hearth of your love, light all
the lamps against the night. Hard to forgive
the way he slammed the door in your face,
his implacable need to travel, that he
wouldn't listen when you said *Stay*.

Blood Orange

At midnight in her kitchen
redolent with the scent of citrus,
I scrape the zest of oranges,
making bread for mother's tea.
The grater's steel rosettes bite
thick rind, scratching
pale gold sawdust in a pile.
I am careful: those sharp fangs
can chew a finger raw.

At my feet, Chloe twitches
her paws, chasing dream rabbits.
I can hear, above the clock's relentless tock,
my mother moaning softly in her sleep,
and I wonder if, in dreams, she escapes
her chair and like the dog, runs free.

Ah! To the grater's teeth,
any flesh is meat—
the orange's or mine.
I suck a torn knuckle, but too late:
one red drop colors pale shreds
on the cutting board.
I fold the rind into rich batter,
blood and all,
an offering to intemperate
and hungry fate.

Family Restaurant

Sisters, I'd guess, by those long oval
faces and Modigliani necks rising like pale
stalks from identical black jackets, eat
antipasto with the elegant zest of young
animals—all slim-fingered precision and muted
chewing—while holding up cell phones, texting
with avid concentration the way belles
at cotillions once fluttered fans.
All the while a silver-haired woman,
surely grandma, sits across from them
silently picking at her house salad,
more alone in their company than I,
a spy scribbling lines on a napkin,
sipping wine at my table for one.

Word Search

Not to be confused with the fun hunt,
the beguiling search for a word to replace *skin*,
for instance,

where I wonder, do I want the naked connotation of flesh,
or pelt, hide, husk, rind, the scum on a cold
coffee cup?

No, this is the desperate trip among twisted neurons
for words gone missing from the tip
of my tongue,

when blanks replace a face's name, or as today, the kind
of crimped black wool that trimmed my sister's coat.
I know

the right word lurks, worry the skein of possibilities:
mohair? mouton? shearling? karakul? No, all
are wrong.

There's just a space where the exact word once lived,
and a deeper emptiness: Sally's dead, can't
help me.

The more elusive my prey, the more frantic I become,
but then, just as I'm dumping Alpo from the can—thank God!
It's Persian lamb.

Second Wind

Don't know what to make of this spate,
sudden squall of poems flooding my dry
arroyo, jostling for space on the page,
sometimes three or four a day. I'm reminded
of Yeats in his dotage, elixir of monkey glands
fizzing his veins, busily plumbing *the foul rag
and bone shop of the heart.* I haven't his art,
but gratefully embrace what I'm given: the crisp

of dry leaves crushed under my boots   crow
call   a certain shade of blue   cat stretched
on the mantel   alphabet serendipity   old wounds
mortality's hissed alarm   carroteggplantmeloncorn
kaleidoscoped in grocery bins   needle prick
blood's crimson   love in its various guises. All

set words humming, all make me fumble
for pen and anything to write on: coiled receipt
fished from my purse, lipsticked napkin, electric
bill back, this ruled tablet—I'm that frantic
to get it all out, higgledy-piggledy without rhyme
or even reason. Ill portent or second wind?
No matter. This instant's maybe all I have.

Ready

All day she's prepared welcome—made up the bed
with fresh sheets hot and crisp from her iron,
set an extra place at the table, basted the roast,
muttered potential opening lines. She knows it's pathetic,
but can't resist checking the clock obsessively, plucking
the drapes aside to peek out at the empty street, wondering
if he'll really show. Then just as hope trickles down the drain,
something in the atmosphere shifts—a whispered displacement
of air—and her poem is there on the doorstep, shuffling
from foot to foot in the cold, juggling a sheaf of tulips,
bottle of cabernet, and trying on smiles.
As the streetlights flick on, he rings her bell, and in the face
of that crooked grin, all she meant to say scatters in the wind
like a flock of startled rooks. Wordlessly, she folds
him into her arms, breathes in the spice of his cologne
she remembers waking to all those years ago.

II. Seasonings

Seasonings

Entering Penzeys shop, where the air, thick
with the scent of mingled spices, is almost
too heavy to breathe, I close my eyes, sniff
cardamom, turmeric, fenugreek, mint,
imagine a souk in Tunis or Tripoli, then allow
a whiff of cilantro, adobo, chipotle pepper, cumin
to drift me south to a bodega in Cancun or Mazatlan,
and at last, let cinnamon, nutmeg and vanilla pull
me back to my mother's Christmas kitchen,
where we rolled and cut cookies thin as cellophane.

And now I think, too, how the earth's turning
traces our times of sowing, growing, reaping,
lying fallow, and how its equinoctial passages
change and teach, seasoning each of us.

The best time of day

is just on the cusp between darkness and light,
the moment night loses its grip and day gathers
itself to begin again—this instant of transition.

In this shadow hour the first thing to see
is how moonset's pewter gleam resurrects trees,
pulls the sky's cold black away from branches' living
black. And the first thing to hear is silence:
crickets, katydids cease rasp and saw, peepers stop
trilling lust songs, and the last raccoon, clever
hands sore from clanging garbage can lids,
has trundled home to rest. All creatures sleep
but you—bears in their dens, foxes curled
nose to tail in their lairs, the thrush's first
tentative chirp still moments away.

Now is the best time to rise and watch
the day's geography draw itself on the map.

Contrary to all expectations

the best awakening is not to a lover's
hardness pressed against your back,
but rather to a poem's wingflutter
tickling brainstem to life, rousing
you to another kind of eagerness: words
yelling *Write! Quick, before the dream*
retreats into night's dim mysteries, its vague
memory only a teasing refrain.

Better, too, than the screaming alarm
or sun prying eyelids open, this insistent
call to arms. To start your day craving
a pen and yellow legal pad even more
than his touch, coffee, that first cigarette:
this is the meaning of heat.

False Spring

On the first day the mercury hit 50,
tidal waves of teenagers poured
from the high school, spraying laughter bright
and high on the street. Into their eddies—carefully—
a woman waded, head bent against the crash
of spring voices, gnarled hands clutching
her drugstore catch. Oblivious to robins and jagged
crocus spikes, she wore wool—brave, defiant scarlet—
a warning beacon among the Jordan Almond colors of the young.
Mauve, pink, lime and yellow, spindrift energy
crackling the air, they parted for her prow,
needing more years to read her red semaphore:
You can never be too warm, it said.
Wait. It's only March.

Le Chaim!

Snowdrops, deceptively fragile, spear
up through ice crusts, signal forsythia
to foam hillsides yellow, maple buds
to swell, unfurl and birth green, lilacs
to purple the dooryard, tulips
to release their crisp, vegetal scent,
irises to flaunt extravagant frills.
Nothing can resist spring's importuning,

not even me. It's as if my gray winter
mood's an affront to all this color,
and I'm compelled to use a brighter palette,
even though my springs are numbered. Cheering
to know, our seasons over, the calendar
will still unroll its pages, no matter what.

Violet Boys

Aides from the group home
shuttle back and forth to the van
in pouring rain, help the men down,
point them toward the door the way
you'd aim a wind-up toy at a wall.

The guys who call Violet House home
negotiate slick sidewalks like dancing
bears or astronauts with lead in their boots,
one slow foot at a time, carefully lifted.
Pointless to call the fate that made them children
in old men's clothes blessing or curse.
This is how they came or have become.

Most of the Violet boys home in
on the rectangle of yellow light,
oblivious to thunder rumbles,
lightning zig-zagging above trees fluffed
with spring flowering, but one wavers
to a stop, lifts his pale moon face
ecstatically to the deluge,
sings a wordless hymn of bliss.

Easter 2010

All the food in my fridge is dead.
A few mummified peas rattle across the freezer floor.
General Tso's remains grow a white beard
in their cardboard coffin, and the last Kirby cuke
slides relentlessly toward rot, thin skin just
holding back the flood of liquid pith and seeds.
Ancient gravy has become a dry and fissured
wasteland preserved in plastic. Lettuce leaves, brown
at their furled rims, are translucent, thin as an old woman's skin.
Even the maraschino cherries have lost their shine.
Brown sludge coats the crisper's bottom, and I mourn
those orphaned carrots, limp celery ribs, shriveled apples
whose bodies have returned to primordial ooze.
No neat "dust to dust" here—just the awful stink of decay.

In the tomb of my fridge, those peas will never
plump up into tender emerald pillows, the General
will not rise again to bite my tongue, nor cukes
return to crunchiness, gravy to its silken youth.
I shroud the tiny corpses in black body bags,
consign them to the trash. In the morning,
not even the racoons will touch them.

Home Making

I can't keep house.
Scrubbed, gleaming woodwork
smears with jammy handprints as I watch,
and dustballs big as tumbleweeds
lead nomadic lives beneath my bed.
Archaeologists could plumb
the secret strata of my closets,
discover dead worlds.

Yet I delight in order:
I want to snap
sundried sheets on all the beds,
press my face in fragrant
piles of matching towels,
sniff lemon oil's tart, astringent tang,
see daisies jump
from dinnerplate mirrors and the bowls
of silver spoons.

But since I can't keep house,
I polish words.

A Taste of Things to Come

Eighty degrees at 8 a.m., smoky
sky sullen as a convenience store clerk,
not even a whisper of breeze
to tease damp tendrils away from my nape.
The cats are cranky, splay themselves like small
rugs on the cool stone floor. A lone mosquito
whines like a dentist's drill, scratching
the ire sizzling under my skin.

I'm sitting in front of the box fan
in my underwear when a clutch
of Jehovah's Witnesses knocks.
Admirable, the strength of faith
that sends them to me in this heat,
but it's too late. I'm beyond saving.

Happy Trails

Opening Credits

I fed on Wild West romance as a child—singing
cowboys galloping on silver-saddled palominos,
Laura Ingalls Wilder cozy in her little house.
Toy six-shooters strapped to skinny hips,
I rode our development's paved prairies
on a saddle-bagged bike named Blackie,
dreamed myself in gingham, growing up
a cowboygirl unfenced under starry skies.

Dissolve

Sixty years pass, and I'm Montana bound
in the back seat of a Kia Sorrento. Sunscreened,
sandaled, munching Doritos, led by our GPS,
we do the Badlands, Deadwood, the Devils Tower's
exclamation point at the end of the plains' long sentence,
a bison steak, hot shower, clean motel sheets waiting
to soothe old bones at the end of each day's trail.

Zoom In

A perfect Ansel Adams moon, alone in a sky
not dark enough for stars yet, illuminates the peaked
horizon beyond our cabin's deck, whose edge juts
over Wyoming foothills like a liner's prow
above the waves. Silence rules this ocean of sand
and agate-bearing stone. No night bird cry,
coyote howl, mouse-rustle in the grass, not even
the stream's music penetrates the empty air.
We swim in its depths, suck it into our pores,
drink in its gift with every breath.

Fade to Black

Struck dumb by this implacable land,
I wonder how they did it, those pioneers,
ask what dreams propelled them, hearts in their mouths,
to climb the Powder River Pass a thousand feet
high in ox-drawn Conestogas, to die young
in a smoke-choked hut or scrape a snake-bit
living from such unforgiving ground.

Mount Rushmore

In the Black Hills superlatives get old, their meanings
blurred with repetition. And yet, despite such splendor,
I have no wish to visit Mount Rushmore, doubt the presidents'
stony flesh will thrill me—too many years of watching Cary Grant
dangle from Lincoln's nose, I guess. But picked out in polished
white against brown mountain, Gutzen Borglum's boys astound.

Amazing how men like my son-in-law's uncle, hoisted high
in bosun's chairs to fragile scaffolds, honeycombed the rock
with boreholes, blasted all those years. Today the busts'
hooded eyes haunt, seem alive and somehow sad.
Teddy's glasses, just suggested by a carved and arcing
nose piece, appear to sparkle in the sun as he looks out
over sweaty tourists in Hawaiian shirts and baseball caps
licking cones, taking selfies, texting friends back home.

Travelers' Advisory

If you are a deer reading this,
first let me say: Stay away!
Don't cross the highway where thickets
cozy up to the road on both sides
of Route 6. It's an outdoor
abattoir for fawn and doe.

Just yesterday an SUV glowing
like a flame and big as a tank
mowed down one of your own.
And mind you, she saw it coming,
picked up speed, bunched
her haunches for one last bound.
But the driver, with plenty of time
to stop, slammed her in mid-leap,
and she flew in a russet arc, fell,
slim legs running crazily in place.
Phone still glued to an ear,
her killer never even slowed.

I tell you this because, despite
the havoc you wreak on my corn, scat
dropped on the patio, apples poached
from my trees, your large, wild presence—
liquid eyes just inches from my window—
makes me believe.

Oak Park Farmers' Market

Saturdays, the church parking lot blossoms
into a tent city of plenty. We vow we'll just
pick up some lettuces and ramps for salad, new
potatoes, one bunch of French breakfast radishes
to slice and eat on buttered pumpernickel. But greed
flicks its tongue, and suddenly our bags bulge
with acacia honey, veined cheeses, sour cherries,
wild black raspberries, baby pattypan squash,

and of course we're compelled to eat the famous
donuts, still hot from the vat, that church cooks
pass up from basement windows into our waiting hands.
Skins dusted with cinnamon sugar, crisp to the bite,
yield to fluff—so good we could eat a dozen
just standing there, fat glistening on our lips.

The El

Commuters pressed thigh to thigh in silver tubes
that ply colored routes to the Loop just call it *the train.*
So mundane for them to fly high above the trees and two-flats
of suburban neighborhoods, flash past a stranger's kitchen
window, that they frown over tattered paperbacks or nap,
pay no mind to the bathrobed woman we rocket past,
making her tea slop in its saucer, walls vibrate. But I stare
at this frame clipped from the film of her life, captivated.

The El—wild and dangerous as carnival tilt-a-whirls
that spun me as a child—is my once-a-summer roller
coaster, hurtling the curves, jerking us side to side
chink-chunk in unison. Now grown, I suppress
the unseemly urge to scream and thrust arms
in the air, hide my foolish pleasure in the ride.

Joy Ride

Flecks of pepper dotting the sky's cream, birds
rise and wheel as one over the shopping
mall, Kmart, cinema complex converted
to a church, Toys "R" Us and asphalted acres
planted with cars and rusty pickup trucks. Surely
some necessity compels their flight—
search for a safe roost or food—but today
they seem to fly purely for their own amusement.

Staring out the restaurant window, spoon poised
between bowl and lips, I watch the flock do loop-
the-loops, barrel rolls and dives, flick back
and forth in tumbling Immelman turns, split, regroup
into one great round—thousands of them—in a dance
so exuberant I watch until my soup grows cold.

Out of the blue

or somewhere nearer, words rain down today,
splashing puddles, shrieking joy for no reason
except their own pleasure, the way cats chase
tails or a mare goes in a moment from grazing
to gallop when put out to grass: pleather pumice
penitential titmouse sphincter foxglove trash
dander abracadabra mammoth fortissimo hawk
fractious tremblor rumble salacious dishabille
wanton snatch palimpsest dreadnaught twang
wrinkle tinkle rhombus thrum rhumba googolplex
rutabaga thin-skinned egregious naked thigh
velvet wine impoverished pang mendacity lux
maniacal tickle lemon verbena horsefeathers wimple
dimple melamine shine rash clash logorrhea.

Meteor Shower

At midnight the dark is palpable,
and leaving the kitchen's glow to feel my way
outdoors is like bumping into a block
of polished stone. Pupils
grow so big I think they will explode,
their black merging with the sky.

A gibbous moon lurks behind the eaves,
and summer stars, so long dead,
blink and glitter ancient light
down through space and time.
Fireflies send coded messages
of who knows what to their mates.

Stillness slows my pulse until the neighbor's
boy guns up the hill in his tricked-out truck,
bass up full like a battering ram.
I want to run after him, snarling madly,
and savage his tires with my fangs,
but he's already out of range.

My neck aches, tired bones grinding
as I lift my face, seeking the Perseids.
Presently, a single bolt of light arcs and dies
like a cigarette flicked from a car window.
A beat, then three dots explode in delicate
sprays of silent fireworks.

I lie down on the driveway, spread like a starfish,
feeling the sun's stored heat on my back. As the cold
stones flare and wink out, I wish for peace, the return
of reason, long lives for my children, a good night's
sleep. And I wish time would suspend its animation,
this moment stretching out forever.

Coup d'état

This summer poison ivy invaded the myrtle,
ternate leaves so stealthy under the groundcover
that, weeding, I didn't notice until the blisters
formed, oozed their itchy juices, made me rake
my flesh like a penitent, spreading pain. Hands
swelled for a hellish week or so, but now
I know to keep my distance, let it grow.

Like all wildness, the ivy's won and climbs exultantly
up the gutter, drapes itself over the door, lying
in wait like a python, it's vines stretching to touch
my face. Crimson now, in autumn, very pretty
in its own malignant way, as if it wants to coax
me to lave my skin in its oily richness—
and I'm afraid.

Grist

The harvest depends on remembering
the exact blue of shadows, screech
of nails on the blackboard, how the wind
twists and makes everything fly,
butter's salty unguence, desire's hot
palm pressing your back, the scent
of your mother's perfume, and the point
where they all intersect.

Couple

Long beyond the time their neighbors
turned stark skeletons, black against the sky,
two maples side by side at the bottom
of my hill still radiate: the taller, scarlet,
his companion an orangey gold.
I like to think they've mated, grown
together fifty years or more, patiently
enduring the vicissitudes of time, weather,
blight, the daily grind. These trees
have put behind them petty quarrels, imagined
slights, and despite a certain achiness of limb
and root, the boredom of proximity,
they're still hot for each other, ignite
at the slightest touch of light.

For Martha

the last passenger pigeon, d. 1914

How did it feel to be the last of your kind,
to wake one morning to an empty nest,
no mate answering your amorous coos,
no familiar shapes perched in the hedges,
no creature speaking the tongue you knew?

Once you flew in migratory clouds
so thick they darkened the sun at noon,
now all gunned down but you, the one
they saved, caged and fed thirty years in a zoo,
then stuffed, mounted and displayed.

In our defense, it must be said we tried hard,
the year you died, to eradicate our own kind,
too, at Verdun, the forests of Argonne
and in muddy trenches all along the Western Front.

Premonition

The moon is out of sorts tonight.
Worry lines vee her brow, right eye has a wild,
uncertain gaze, mouth's O shows…not fear
exactly…let's just say preoccupied concern,
and a jaundiced haze smears the clean edges
of her face. We'd like to blame her strange
expression on her time of month (just a phase
she's going through) because although she's
neither red nor blue, she's not quite ripe.
But, as a sudden grimace intimates the first
appalling pain when a heart explodes inside
its cage, tonight her lunar landscape looks
as if she's been unpleasantly surprised
by our foolishness below.

Every so often

after Shakespeare's Sonnet 73

anxiety chews its leash, fangs bare
and slavering, the day's calm, ruined.
Only leaden tocsins clang. No angel choirs
sing in the echoing halls of a mind where
once contentment oozed honey. Too late
now to shore up defenses, recoup the
lost peace. If only I could snare sweet
hope, but she flies from my grasp like birds
wheel up from trees. I remember how she sang.

Autumnal Equinox

Earth tilts us away and light turns stingy,
reluctant to start its day early, stay late,
put in overtime as it does in generous summer.
As this diminishment approaches, like bears know
to bulk up on salmon and berries, I grow greedy
for fat, butter toast more lavishly, fry rashers,
trying to wrap their heat around my bones.
We all slow down, dig in to endure the dark.
In this time of thin light, my parents, too,
tilted away from the sun, cold husks turned to dust.
No wonder the ancients feared this waning.
No wonder Goethe cried out *More light!* as he died.

Bowing to the Inevitable

Finally turning the dial, I set the beast
of this house humming, heart ticking
away, bare metal ribs thrusting hot
breath up from the depths of its chest.
I'm loathe to awaken his ravenous
appetite that last winter ate
by the ton kilowatts I starved to buy.
But tonight, despite resolve to tough
it out, my creature need for heat betrays.
No matter how many sweaters, shawls
and woolen socks I layer, countless bowls
of fatty stew I consume, nor how many mugs
of steaming tea I swill, the cold's won out
as it always does and always will.

Lessons

Winter of busted pipes, no running water, teaches
thrift—not a drop from gallons carted home
wasted. We learn to boil peas and potatoes in the same
pot, scrub the sink with its dregs.

Once I fantasized being raised a long-skirted
child, riding a dappled pony alongside the family
buckboard, picking wildflowers, carrying yoked
pails from a spring to water our mules at dusk.

But in this season of drought, I'm worn out.
Arms muscled up and aching from toting jug
after jug from car to kitchen, two clutched
in each hand, I learn that dream is no fun,

discover I can't stand to go dirty like that calico
girl trekking west across the desert, must
bathe daily standing in a rubber tub,
then lug its scummy run-off to flush the toilet.

Sleepless

Tonight as you begin the slow drift down
into oblivion's jeweled sea and blessed
relief, some inner alarm—a pang,
or synapse sparking too brightly—snaps
you back to the surface, and you're in Somnia,
that dreamless land you inhabit alone,
where eyes dilate against the dark and sheets
knot from sweaty, restless thrashing.

And let me tell you, nothing is lonlier
than lying awake while the whole house
curls under quilts—even the winter mice
in its walls at rest from their scurries
and gnawings—all asleep except you,
your busy mind, your pounding heart.

Winter Solstice

for Lynn Merriken 1943-2011

The stark architecture of trees
perfectly limned in black and white
there in the Notch, where snow
coated only one side of the trunks
as if it had been rulered onto the bark:
a precision so lovely I gasped
and swerved into the passing lane.
Small gifts matter now, on the year's
shortest day when news of an old friend's
death snaps mortality into sharp focus.
I mourn the loss of light and time,
her empty chair, the fact we lived
in the same city and never knew.
Near the end, maybe, life pares down
to essentials: positive and negative
space, patterns delineated, erased.

First of the Season

We wake to a changed world,
its softened, serene landscape whispering
us back to childhood: branches cottoned
like kindergarten art, drifts waiting
for flung-down bodies to make angels
and just right for packing, pitched battles.
Remember when a snowball shattered,
sifting its chill down the back of your neck,

and that was the worst that could happen?
No heart attacks from shoveling snow, no
broken hips, and none of us had heard
of hypothermia or homeless men found
frozen beneath the viaduct. Just for today,
lace up your skates, make cocoa, revel.

III. On Looking into Gray's Anatomy

Manufacturer's Instructions

Just relax. Don't be afraid. Poems will seldom
hurt you, and when taken as directed,
side effects are generally benign and minimal.
At first you may experience brief bouts
of dizziness, blurred vision or confusion,
so don't drive or operate toothed and dangerous
machinery until you know how their words
will affect you. Warning: in rare cases, readers
have reported more serious complications.
If you have difficulty breathing or bizarre
dreams, where you're lost in an alien forest
whose trees reach out with malevolent intent,
discontinue use and take two aspirin.
In the morning, I'll call to you.

Anatomy I: Introductory Lecture

Today, boys and girls, we begin
our study of the body's poetry.
Here, you'll see how its systems play
their roles in life's intricate machine.

Some of you will quail at the prospect
of dissecting jarred cats, lambs' brains,
your own eccentricities, but only by slicing
and prizing apart can we examine
our brief and vulnerable struts.

We begin with the essential cell and its replication.
Later, when you're older, you'll learn the organs
of generation. Then on to our underpinnings: bones
and the muscles that move them, including joy,
desire, grief and rage, with some attention to guilt.

Next, our engines and transmission systems:
the brain and its busy messages, blood's dark
secrets, the heart's great, fallible pump,
the lungs, each precious breath.

Last, we'll consider what feeds us—
how we chew, digest, excrete every bite
life sends our way—including, but not limited
to, how the moon, each leaf and tree
frog, cedar waxwing, ball of dust all
inform the "organs of special sense"
we use to imagine the world.

And remember this: to understand the body's
comedies and dramas, attention must be paid
when the world cries *Connect* and illuminates
the incandescent mystery of how we are all,
children, all, greater than the sum of our parts.

The problem with color

is naming it true,
giving due respect to tint
and hue, of course, but also
to scent, taste, mood and similes
learned in English 102.

Take this spring wine held
up to the light. I might
well think it looks precisely
like a healthy woman's pee,
bright and clear, but who
in their right mind would drink?

Amber? Topaz? No, more like straw,
and I could swear I saw a hint
of celadon or mint, perhaps.
Nothing raw as bile, God knows,
nor green as milky jade;
no glint of lime.

Say sunlight pale on April grass,
or gold and green distilled,
passed through finest net,
and you'll almost get it, but not
quite. So, should anyone care to ask,
I'll simple tell them white.

Grammar Class

Wish I could diagram this life sentence
the way Miss Kiley taught us in tenth grade—
she of the improbably cantilevered bosom
and bad jokes. But I digress. (She'd take off points for this.)

My friends had no patience for teasing
apart a sentence's knotted strands, but I loved
how you could chart the words' pure
purposes, divide the line of their meaning
perpendicularly into subject, verb and object,
how that line sprouted
slanting adjective shoots like radish roots,
the way prepositional phrases' crooked
branches dangled, their caterpillar legs scurrying
the sentence along.

Above all, I took comfort in the diagram's
reliable structure inviting us to unclutter
ambiguity—each part of speech
assigned a place, everything under control.

Talk Shop

In the language store, dried vocal
cords hang in strands like tendrils
of a man o' war. Tongues
float in jars—pale peach slices—
spongy, but tough to chew, and
larynxes tied in clacking bunches
castanet in the breeze of our passing.

The pigtailed clerk sells freeze-dried
fricatives in packets. Plosives come
in atomizers, ready to spray in faces.
Glottal stops, caught live in the Kalahari,
collide in their pens against the wall.
(You can hear them clicking and
clocking excitedly at feeding time.)

Little tins of umlauts, tildes and cedillas
only cost a dollar, and this week lazy
drawls from Charleston and choice Scottish
burrs, with their rough, phlegmy edges,
are on sale—a connoisseur's delight.
For flavor, try a Texas twang, bit of liquid Hindi,
or a sibilant Catalonian lisp (complete with gestures).

In a fix? The old man who owns the place
will custom-mix windbags of bilge and bromides.
Clichés are cheap, and so is twaddle, but the sounds
he clearly loves the best (kept under the counter
bound in silk, away from all the rest) will cost you
dearly: for comfort, buy a Mother Tongue; for all
the innocence you've lost, the soft lallation of a baby's cry.

Body Language

Listen. Your body is talking to you.
In the rollicking hurdy-gurdy
of its burp, hiss and gurgle,
it speaks of the fun of digestion,
tells bathroom jokes. But it can moan
the dull thrum of ache, yelp pain's
acid twinge. And in its breathy sighs,
your body is saying *Look! I'm alive.*

Quiet. Your body's on stage, singing
its pleasures: delight's tickled-pink
chuckles, gut tuba oompah-ing
polkas of joy. Its toe-tapping
begs you to rise, join in life's
endlessly circling hora. Its throat
cries *Drink deep, take every chance.*
Look ma, it says, *I can dance!*

Pay attention. Your body is strumming
its hungers. Empty belly's echo
calls for sustenance. Longing's slow
arpeggios fall like water, and lust's
itchy staccato plucks, its snare rasp
fizzing the blood in your veins.
Just listen. Hear how your heart's
drum thumps to the beat of *I want.*

Be still. Your body is whispering
clues, something within giving
a nudge to tune your ear to its infinite
symphony, playing awake and asleep.
Hush. Your body is saying
I'm doing my job, tuned to your needs.
For the moment, all systems are go.

How to Worship

Begin with your feet. Observe
their marvelous architecture, see
how the tarsals and metatarsals fit
in an intimate jigsaw,
rise like a cairn
stacked at the edge of a trail
in Nepal: calcus, astralagus,
cuboid, navicular, the four
cuneiform bones.

Now let your eye follow the path
down to the phalanges
and pause.
Roll that word on your tongue:
phalanges. Those little toes,
so suckable,
huddled together for warmth
down there at the very tip
of your body's South Pole.

Study your feet with wonder,
think how their delicate
structure supports your full weight,
day after day,
and praise them.

Head of Aphrodite (circa 1st century)

Only this mute stone, spot-lit and pedestalled
in the exhibit hall, remains for our inspection.
True, by today's slim standards, her face is too fleshy
to be beautiful. All the same, we can sense the slow
roll of her hips and understand the ancients' veneration
of this goddess, wellspring of procreation, pleasure, joy.

Then, suddenly, she's dangerous, and one
look impels some well-meaning Christian zealot
to incise a cross on her forehead, give this pagan
deity an overlay of new faith. But it gets worse.
This man, or someone later, quite literally defaces
her, and in her broken nose, gouged-out eyes,
lips chiseled to ribbons, we can read a darker motive.

Studying her devastation, I imagine a man
who felt enslaved by passion, so disgusted
by his own lust he felt compelled to erase
her allure, silence her voice, blind her knowing
gaze, savage this hunk of stone.
At any rate, he failed. Even today, her ruined
features vibrate with the power of the body's welcome.

At First Sight

Inanimate and pure as unappled Eve,
she impales your heart
the moment your eye slides
across her blond belly
and you read the bookmatched
Rorschach of its Sitka spruce.
One look at polished rosewood steamed
to fit her deeply female form, her slender
neck, its ivory frets, embellishments
of ebony and nacre scraped from abalone
shells, and a plangent longing stirs.
The second you touch, feel how perfectly
her inward curve fits your thigh,
you're hooked before the first strum.

On Looking into *Gray's Anatomy*

The Back

In Figure 213, the back of a man
is unskinned, muscles laid bare,
trapezius, latissimus dorsi dissected.
How lovely these intricate twinings,
smooth sheathes reaching over and up
from the spine.
I recall watching you take off your shirt
in the sun and loving the play of those muscles
as you bent from the waist,
straining to shift a boulder.

The Tongue

Seen up close the tongue is fairly
disgusting—a muscled slug,
its papillae, with taste buds embedded,
covered by a scaly epithelium
thinner than skin.
But for all its ugliness, the tongue
is exquisitely sensitive, and such fun
when it licks nipples and lips.

The Brain

Just look at the possibilities of its parts:
imagine the cerebellum tolling the hour,
a diva receiving bravos for her medulla
oblongata, Michelangelo carving a marble
Pia Mater for the Pope, or spelunkers
exploring the Fissure of Rolando while
a hippocampus lolls in the riverbank mud.
Now picture all of us writhing
lustily in a gyrus fornicatus, to fornix.
And at the end, we each become a corpus
callosum ferried to thalamus.

Fingerprints

In its ability to discriminate, Spell-Check's
a dismal failure, indistinguishable to it
the difference between ball and bawl,
or the bill of a bird, cap, my son's name.
And no wonder: how could a machine
understand what we mean to mean?

But a thumb's topography—its friction
ridges mounded or steepled like isobars
on a weather map, its gorgeous spiraled
whorls and central pocket loops—defines exactly
who last raised that axe, jimmied the door,
made off with the family jewels,

and, ambiguity erased, we can see who cradled
a pink cup in both hands, perhaps blew
to cool its steaming tea, and who came slick
from the womb, whose arms opened, gathered
him in to her breast—each story, each little
life unique in the truest sense of the word.

Nighthawks

Three hatchet-faced figures focus our attention—
two picked out against the dark outside the diner's
plate glass window, counterman by lemon light—
but I am drawn to the mystery of the woman in red.
Exhausted at this late hour, she looks like death,
her pallor under the harsh and unforgiving light
accentuated by a slash of crimson lipstick,
the shine of her dress, fall of orange hair. Everything
about her is attenuated: nose, cheekbones, clavicle's
declivity, long arms, as if she's barely hanging on.

Once she might have been a dancer, but tonight she belongs
to the man in the gray fedora with nose like a beak
and a raptor's empty eyes. One hand almost touches
his. The other holds a small green square she contemplates
with hopeless resignation—perhaps a note or compact? No,
I suspect it's cash. And doesn't that change everything?

Where Everything Happens

Somewhere on the border of riddle and answer,
Mystery is sneaking a peek,
and lost on the corner of truth and mendacity,
Memory is calling her mother.

Somewhere on the brink of might and action,
Sloth is taking a nap,
and pacing the verge of should and indifference,
Duty is hedging her bets.

Somewhere on the margin of ripeness and rot,
Hunger is holding her breath,
and just on the threshold of ugly and plain,
Mercy is weighing her options.

Somewhere on the fence of stop and yes,
Desire is playing for time,
and see—right at the line between you and me—
Love is changing the sheets.

And somewhere on the edge of maybe and never,
Hope is packing her bags.

Report

The bullets came to his face,
his cheek, says the nameless
Libyan student describing how
her uncle died under sniper fire,
as if they—the bullets—were
soft kisses.

Imagine this man walking
a rubbled street, sweet scent
of cardamom still on his breath,
afternoon heat raising tiny
diamonds of sweat at his hairline.
In the blink
between being and nonbeing
perhaps he is thinking of his wife
grinding chickpeas for dinner,
and how her flesh will taste later.

From a rooftop the gunman's eye
sights a cheekbone in the crosshairs,
fires, sees the neat red rosettes
blossom, their hail dimple the dust.
Dead before the rifle's crack comes,
the uncle slumps to the curb,
a bag of rags and bone, one
lens starred like a sapphire.

Unveilings

A scarf of cloud and mist drifts across
the shoulders of a distant hill: opaline,
gray, the palest blue, like watered silk.
Wind pulls an edge gently, two-fingered,
undressing dark mounds, a patient
and attentive lover who knows that slowing
the moment makes revelation sweeter.

Under unkind light in the examining room,
I'm told to strip, slip on a paper gown.
It rustles, harsh against bare skin pocked
with cold and fear. The doctor probes my spleen;
flesh winces away from his insistent
press. *Normal*, he says, enters a note,
leaves without even a handshake. I dress.

Memento mori

Those Flemish artists were so sly, beguiling us
with harvest still lifes of plump and glistening fruits—
apples, pears and cherries heaped in silver urns—
inviting us to sink our teeth into ripeness, feel
juices spurt, run down our chins. But in every
one something mutters of decay: the tiny worm
emerging, a desiccated rind, guttering candle
flames, a fly. The signs are always there, reminding.

When I wind up the mountain road vibrant
with October foliage to visit my dearest friend,
see how her flesh has been pared to the bone,
the sharp planes of her skull thrust to the surface,
all of her eaten away but the essential shining
core, I know winter's not far behind.

The Great Debate

I ponder the thin line between need and want
while trying on a pair of fleece-lined, round-
toed slippers so comfortable they make
my aching bunions moan with pleasure, my toes
sing alleluias, then put them aside:
an unnecessary indulgence.

Need is easy to define: the cry of a lost
child wandering department store aisles
in search of her mother, the rumble of an empty
belly, abscessed tooth throbbing for relief,
strong locks on the door, pure water,
clean sheets.

And I see the beauty of simplicity, long
to expunge clutter, strip life down to its minimum
so that what really matters can shine.
Now's the time, I tell myself, to focus on what
I truly cherish, absolutely need to see
me through to the end.

But oh, the call of want is strong! It screams
More, please: oysters on the half shell, a jelly
doughnut, just one more cigarette, new red
dress, a lover inappropriately young and doting.
And already I'm regretting the loss
of those incredible slippers.

My Body I Dispose

"Now, now that the sun hath veiled his light and bid the world goodnight, to the soft bed, my body I dispose. But where shall my soul repose? Dear, dear God, even in thine arms."

from *Evening Hymn* by Henry Purcell

How will they dispose of me, my slim leavings—
just a huff of gray dust in a cardboard box?
Will my children plant me in the churchyard
garden near my parents' long-leached powders,
or say *No, let's set her free, sprinkle her on a lake,*
maybe toss her from a mountaintop in Maine,
or better yet, from a Pennsylvania knoll (so much
easier to climb and closer)?

Secretly, I wish they would retrieve my hollow
rounds of vertebrae and bumpy finger knuckles
(as I longed to do when mother died but lacked
the nerve) and string them like beads to wear
necklaced against their skins, the way I warmed
their tiny forms, held them close inside all
that time before I pushed them into life, set them
free to breathe on their own.

Last Wishes

As I lie dying, pipe Garrison Keillor's voice
into my ear—so quiet, calm, uninflected, filled
with the infinite resignation such departures
require. Let him recall for me the simple pleasures
of rhubarb pie, poetry, fine old hymns, Lake Woebegone's
follies and sly ironies. Have him sing by my bed
so I can float my old voice over the rumbling
swell of his baritone, harmonize one more time to *Plaisir
d'amour.* We'll take our sweet time on the chorus,
no need to rush now the end is near. Yes,
I could go gently, hand enfolded in his big
warm paw, lulled by his murmurous drone,
all of us, my darlings, smiling and waving goodbye
as my boat pulls away from shore.

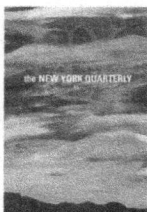

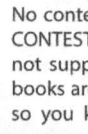
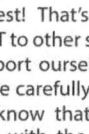

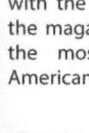

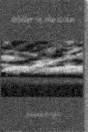

www.ingramcontent.com/pod-product-compliance
Lightning Source LLC
Chambersburg PA
CBHW022013080426
42733CB00007B/585